W9-COB-633

Writer's Little Instruction Book

# GETTING PUBLISHED

### PAUL RAYMOND MARTIN

**WRITER'S DIGEST BOOKS**
Cincinnati, Ohio
www.writersdigest.com

**Writer's Little Instruction Book: Getting Published.** © 2005 by Paul Raymond Martin. Manufactured in the United States of America. All rights reserved. No part of this book may be reproduced in any form or by any electronic or mechanical means including information storage and retrieval systems without permission in writing from the publisher, except by a reviewer, who may quote brief passages in a review. Published by Writer's Digest Books, an imprint of F+W Publications, Inc., 4700 East Galbraith Road, Cincinnati, OH 45236. (800) 289-0963. First edition.

Visit our Web site at www.writersdigest.com for information on more resources for writers. To receive a free weekly e-mail newsletter delivering tips and updates about writing and about Writer's Digest products, register directly at our Web site at http://newsletters.fwpublications.com.

09  08  07  06  05       5  4  3  2  1

Library of Congress Cataloging-in-Publication Data

Martin, Paul Raymond.
  Writer's little instruction book. Getting published : includes more than 300 secrets and strategies / by Paul Raymond Martin.
     p. cm.
  ISBN 1-58297-343-1 (pbk. : alk. paper)
  1. Authorship–Marketing. I. Title: Getting published. II. Title.
  PN161.M375 2005                                    2004028846
  070.5'2—dc22

Edited by Kelly Nickell
Designed by Lisa Buchanan-Kuhn and Grace Ring
Cover Photography by Al Parrish
Page Layout by Joy Delker
Production Coordinated by Robin Richie

# DEDICATION

**This book is dedicated to developing writers everywhere**
who attend workshops and ask questions, who share their writing and offer
critiques, who offer insights about writing and exchange information. And first
among these are my colleagues at Pennwriters and Second Tuesday.

# ACKNOWLEDGMENTS

Robin Estrin, for her constancy and encouragement.
Jane Friedman, who stuck her neck out in a new job to acquire this book.
Lavern Hall, who will always be my first publisher.
Lisa Kuhn and Grace Ring, who made this a beautiful book with their design.
Kirk Nesset, the best short fiction critiquer I have ever encountered.
Kelly Nickell, who made this a better book with her editing.
Rita Rosenkranz, who negotiated the contract and freed me to write.
Kathie Westerfield, who provided me with a writing haven when I most needed it.

# TABLE OF CONTENTS

# INTRODUCTION: GETTING PUBLISHED

The response to *The Writer's Little Instruction Book: 385 Secrets for Writing Well & Getting Published*, originally released in 1998, was both gratifying and surprising. My little book, adopted by classroom teachers from middle school through college, also became a hit at writers' workshops. While I didn't anticipate so many readers would draw life lessons from it, as well as inspiration and instruction for their writing, the results have been most rewarding. Thus, my little book has grown into a series of three:

*Writer's Little Instruction Book: Inspiration & Motivation*
*Writer's Little Instruction Book: Craft & Technique*
*Writer's Little Instruction Book: Getting Published*

Each volume includes motivational quotes and secrets for effective writing from prominent authors and editors, original aphorisms to keep you focused and on track, anecdotes to illustrate key points related to writing and the writing life, and story starters or publishing strategies to inspire your work when you're stuck or when you just want to try something new.

May your stride be longer returning from the mailbox than on the way to it.

# SELF-EDITING & REWRITING:
## Fail Your Way to Success

# I can't write five words but that I change seven.

—Dorothy Parker, short-story writer and poet

No passion in the world is equal to the passion to alter someone else's draft.

—H.G. Wells, author of *The War of the Worlds*

Once something is down I don't usually change it. I do my rewriting every day. I don't rush to the end as I know some writers do, sort of get the whole story down, and then go back.

—Alice McDermott, author of *Child of My Heart* and *That Night*

The most useful skill a writer can acquire is the ability to **edit one's work** ruthlessly.

➤ Make revision a way of life.

Never allow the **editor in your head** to dampen the emotions in your heart or the enthusiasm in your soul.

➤ Every writer must fashion an editor's hat and keep it close at hand.

➤ The first rule of writing is to write. The second rule of writing is to rewrite. The third rule of writing is the same as the second.

➤ When you finish rewriting a piece, delete the
first paragraph. Now read the story again.
Does it make a difference? If not, try deleting
the first page or the first few pages.

Writers must parent their work
**with tough love**.

> Good writers make more mistakes than poor writers, but never the mistake of not trying to correct mistakes.

**Every** writer exercises the right to write badly. **Good** writers exercise this right until the writing is not too bad.

# The flaws are in **the writing,** not the writer.

> The writer is at the same time the **best judge of his writing, and the worst.**

➤ The key to effective writing is not so much getting words on paper as it is getting words off paper.

➤ The only editor who can change your second-tier writing into first-tier writing is you.

➤ When you are awash in an emotional tidal wave, pour it out on paper. Then distance yourself from it for a time and begin anew, but keep the power of what you wrote earlier.

The longer you let your manuscript sit before editing it, the more it will seem like someone else's work.

> Indulge yourself when you write, but not when you rewrite.

**Write** from the **creative** hemisphere of your brain. **Edit** from the **analytical** hemisphere.

## WEEDS, GLORIOUS WEEDS

A farmer friend of mine says a weed is anything that grows where he doesn't want it to grow. Not long ago, he purchased a tilled field between his place and mine. True to his nature, he promptly removed an apple tree that had, since I was a boy, borne wormy fruit amid the corn, oats, and wheat. The apple tree, no matter how glorious or revered, was growing where my farmer friend didn't want it to grow.

There's a needle-nosed editor in my brain who has much the same attitude.

He routinely waves off my best lines. If it doesn't fit, out it goes, no matter how glorious.

In truth, my farmer friend and my internal editor have it right, at least as it applies to writing. If you really love a passage you've written, almost always it does not belong.

But unlike the old apple tree, you can highlight, click, and save your misplaced glories. Resurrect them when you've found a proper home for them.

Better to write one **superb** sentence than a hundred mediocre ones.

> Whatever you're writing, the work always plays **better in your head** than it does on paper.

➤ Editing demands quality time. Don't short-change yourself in your rush to get a manuscript out the door.

➤ Just because your notebook or computer screen will accept anything doesn't mean your readers will.

➤ Imagine you've just received a call from an editor who would love to use your work—if you can cut the word count in half. (Editors do things like this.)

Imagine you are about to fax your story at **$10 per word**. *Now* edit.

> Wiggle your words this way and that. Dance your way toward what you mean to say.

Rule of thumb for **rewriting:** The beginning is too elaborate and the big scene too skimpy.

## Good writers pretend they are editing someone else's work.

➤ No matter how poorly written a piece, there is always something to build on. No matter how well written a piece, there is always a way to make it better.

➤ Rewrite from several starting points, not just the beginning.

➤ Use short sessions for self-editing, say twenty to thirty minutes.

Try a **different location for editing** than for writing.

Proofread your finished work **at least twice,** especially if you use an electronic spell-checker.

➤ Root out the superfluous and the valueless, lest your flowers be lost among the weeds.

> **Throw out all the stuff the writer needs but the reader doesn't.**

➤ The number of typographical errors varies directly with the creative force of the writing—also with sleep deprivation.

➤ Before you ask, "How can I get it published?" ask, "How can I make it better?"

# STRATEGY:
# WRITE SOMETHING GOOD

The foremost strategy for getting published is to write something good. Developing writers often think about getting published in terms of making the right contacts, researching prospective publishers, and submitting a manuscript in proper format. All those elements, and more, play a role. But when it comes to getting published, nothing matters more than content.

Writing is mostly thinking. Give yourself time to rethink your work. Resist the urge to rush to publish. Rewrite, set the piece aside, rewrite, seek out critiques, rewrite, and rewrite some more. Always send only your absolute best work.

# Cut every sentence to within an **inch of its life.**

## Be miserly toward your words so that editors won't be.

➤ Carving a story is just the opposite of carving a turkey: Cut away everything that isn't essential, and keep the carcass.

➤ Prune your writing as you would a cherry orchard—so that birds might fly through it.

➤ You know you've learned to edit your own work when you can throw out your best writing simply because it doesn't belong.

If a phrase sounds like something you've **heard before**, it will sound that way to the reader, too.

➤ In fiction, "then" is superfluous. The reader knows what is written next happens next.

➤ In real estate, it's "location, location, location." In writing, it's "diction, diction, diction."

**If you get bored** rewriting a part of the story, **pity the reader.** **Dump it.**

## The easy part of writing is deciding what to put in. The difficult part is deciding what to take out.

➤ Ernest Hemingway used the iceberg approach to writing: Nine-tenths of it should be below the surface. The trick is to figure out which 10 percent should be showing.

With each rewrite, you will glean **something of use** in the final draft, or at least eliminate a lot of lousy approximations.

➤ If you use a word processor, save every draft of whatever you're writing. This way you'll be honoring your earlier work, not abandoning it.

# Leave out the parts
## readers skip.

—Elmore Leonard, author of *Mr. Paradise* and
*A Coyote's in the House*

Books are human documents, which means they should have "fingerprints" on them, evidence that a mess went into creating them.

—Carole Maso, author of *Defiance* and *Break Every Rule*

Your manuscript is both good and original; but the part that is good is not original, and the part that is original is not good.

—Samuel Johnson, journalist and author

➤ When you finish rewriting a piece, read it aloud at least twice. Rewrite any sections where you stumble, and add any extra words you used in reading it aloud.

If a name or phrase or passage is **difficult to read aloud**, it also will be **difficult to read silently**.

It's the final draft that creates a **first impression.**

Rewriting is never finished, but **at some point** you have to let it be and **send it out to market.**

➤ While it's true that every writer must develop editing skills, never go to print with only yourself as the editor.

➤ Each rejection slip gives you an opportunity to improve your work. If it no longer pleases you, or if an editor's comments ring true, change the work.

- If additions and deletions are made to respond to critiques rather than to improve the work, the piece becomes "workshopped" and is no longer the author's.

- In editing, the choice is not between "beautiful" and "effective," but rather "beautiful and effective."

Rewriting is the sweat equity of publication.

Thomas Edison said, "I fail my way to success." Writers, too.

# CONFIDENCE:

## No Fair Hiding Stuff in a Drawer

# Writing is the only profession where no one considers you ridiculous if you earn no money.

—Jules Renard, French novelist and playwright

I never had any doubts about my abilities. I knew I could write. I just had to figure out how to eat while doing this.
—Cormac McCarthy, author of *The Orchard Keeper*

Manuscript: something submitted in haste and returned at leisure.
—Oliver Herford, author of *Rubaiyat of a Persian Kitten*

An unpublished manuscript is like an unconfessed sin that festers in the soul, corrupting and contaminating it.
—Antonio Machado, Spanish poet and playwright

> Great writing may be art, but if you don't submit it, who's going to know it?

If you continue to write and rewrite, to **submit and resubmit,** you will publish and republish.

Write as well as you can, say what you have to say, and then **find a market** for your work.

➤ Write what you want, and the money may follow. If it doesn't, at least you wrote what you wanted.

➤ If you write it, there is at least a chance it will be published. If you do not write it, there is no chance it will be published.

Every published writer has produced **some unsalable work.**

# No manuscript in the mail means no check in the mail.

➤ You are an independent businessperson whose product happens to be writing. Like other successful businesspersons, your feet must be running, not planted.

➤ Writing fosters the illusion that you needn't bother with the world. Publication disposes of that illusion.

For the emerging writer, submitting **is at least half the job** of getting published—the dark half.

# WHEN THE CORN
IS TALL

I maintain a month-by-month chart of
when I finish each piece of writing. The
chart helps me track my productivity and
shows my writing pattern. My productivity
varies inversely with the growing season
on my Pennsylvania farm. The taller the
corn, the less I write. I'm most prolific in
the dead of winter.

Try it yourself. List the months of
year along the left margin, then draw a
column for each of the past several years.
In each box, write the title of each unit of
writing you finished in that year and

month. You can define a unit of writing anyway you like: a poem, an article, a short story, or a book chapter. Note the number of pieces you finished each season, as well as the type of work you do during different seasons.

You'll learn something useful about your writing pattern, and what may be keeping you from writing. By the way, if you write most when the corn is tall, let me know how you do that.

Of all the variables in submitting your work, the one over which the writer can exercise **greatest control** is the writing.

➤ No matter how many times you revise a piece, it will always be less than perfect. So make it as nearly perfect as you can at the time—and send it out.

I suppose most editors are **failed writers**—but so are most writers.
—T. S. Eliot, Nobel Prize-winning poet

It is what you read when you don't have to that determines what you will be when you can't help it.
—Oscar Wilde, author of *The Importance of Being Earnest*

We write to taste life twice.
—Anaïs Nin, author of *Delta of Venus*

One of the symptoms of an approaching nervous breakdown is the belief that one's work is terribly important.
—Bertrand Russell, philosopher and author of
*The Analysis of Mind*

➤ In submitting your work, forget fancy fonts and boxed text. Print appearance and layout are editorial prerogatives. You don't have to show an editor what it will look like in print.

Submitting your writing is no
big thing. It's a lot of little things.

## If you're not writing for publication, you're writing a diary.

➤ No writer was ever born published.

➤ Submitting your writing for publication is like e-mail and holiday greeting cards: The more you send the more you receive.

Send all your finished work out to market. No fair hiding stuff in a drawer.

# THE PITCH:

## Never Submit a Story Still Damp with Inspiration

If I wake up thinking about a story I read the night before, **I'm sure to publish that story.**

—Susan Burmeister-Brown, coeditor of *Glimmer Train Stories*

You have to keep writing, keep submitting, and keep praying to the god of whimsy that some editor will respond favorably.

—Peter Benchley, author of *Beast* and *White Shark*

Nothing can destroy the good writer. The only thing that can alter the good writer is death.

—William Faulkner, Nobel Prize-winning novelist

No man but a blockhead ever wrote except for money.

—Samuel Johnson, journalist and author

No matter how strong your query letter is, the **quality of your writing matters most.**

➤ A query letter is a sales pitch; a cover letter is an introduction.

➤ If you write your first query letter really well, you may never have to write another.

➤ In selling your work, don't try to do everything other writers do. Focus on strategies that suit you.

➤ Pay attention to where other writers of your stride are getting published. Are you submitting to those publications?

Selling your work is always
**unfinished business.**

When it comes
to selling anything,
**focus on
benefits** rather
than features.

# STRATEGY:
## WRITE FOR THE MARKET AND NOT

Should you write what the market demands, or should you
write what you want and then find (or create) a market for
your writing?

Both. If you come across an invitation for a kind of writing
that intrigues you, by all means take a flyer on it. But it will
not serve you well to chase a trend. By the time you bring your
writing to market, the trend is likely to have faded. And every
trend was started by a book that did not fit the trend. Better to
write what you care most deeply about and, in doing so, write
so well that you create a market for your work.

➤ Much of submitting your work is serendipity. A matter of the right piece coming to the attention of the right editor at the right time. A matter of the right opportunity coming to the attention of the right writer at the right time.

When you submit your writing, you are in sales. Think accordingly. Act accordingly.

# Never excuse your work
## as "just a draft."

➤ The most effective professional correspondence is not "all business," but person-to-person.

➤ If you send a form letter to an agent or editor, you'll likely get a form reply—one that says no.

When you publish a book, **it's the world's book.** The world edits it.

—Philip Roth, Pulitzer Prize-winning novelist

You may as well write what you want to, because there's no predicting what will sell.

—Judith Guest, author of *Ordinary People*

A good many young writers make the mistake of enclosing a stamped, self-addressed envelope big enough for the manuscript to come back in. This is too much of a temptation to the editor.

—Ring Lardner, sportswriter and novelist

➤ In your cover letter, mention relevant credentials and publishing credits, but don't gush over the quality of your own work.

➤ Respect what others know that you don't—especially about selling your work.

**Never denigrate the publications** in which your work has appeared—especially your early work.

> Copyright does not limit your right to change your work, before or after it is published.

**Do not** attempt to **explain** your work. Either it's on the page, or it's not.

You cannot copyright an idea, only the **expression of an idea**.

➤ Let your story or article sit before you submit it, but only for a day or two, perhaps a week. Then polish and send it off to market.

➤ Copyright is created when the work is created, whether or not the copyright is eventually registered.

➤ If you're writing on spec, draft a marketing plan for each piece as you finish it. Identify three or four prospective markets and the order in which you will approach them.

## Let your writing do the singing, not your cover letter.

## TAKE JOY
## IN BEING A WRITER

Shortly after my first book was published, I was invited by a friend to speak at a workshop for college registrars—not about writing, but about breaking away from the day job to pursue a dream. I told the registrars that you know you're ready to make a change when the telephone rings and you hope it's the dentist calling to confirm your appointment for a cleaning below the gum line—anything, just so it isn't another work-related telephone call.

After my presentation, we held an informal book-signing. Even though my book had nothing to do with college registrars, it did stand as evidence of the possibility of pursuing a dream, and I was mobbed.

The lesson here is twofold: First, when your book is published, open yourself to marketing opportunities that may seem to have nothing to do with your book but everything to do with the pursuit of a dream. Second, you're a writer. All the world envies you.

Take joy in the privilege of being a writer.

Where guidelines permit, simultaneously **submit your work** to several markets.

> Set up a "new markets file" for publications whose guidelines fit your work, even if you have nothing to submit at the time.

## To read a magazine editor's mind, read the magazine.

➤ Read the "best of" anthologies. Note from which magazines and journals the stories are reprinted. Read those magazines and journals.

As you gain publishing credits, submit your work to **evermore competitive markets.**

➤ When submitting your articles and stories to a small-circulation magazine, be sure to mention in your cover letter how you found out about the magazine.

Never submit a story still **damp with inspiration**.

# AGENTS & EDITORS:
## Swim Toward the Bait

Great editors do not discover nor produce great authors; **great authors** create and produce great publishers.

—John Farrar, cofounder of Farrar, Straus & Co.

Did you hear about the editor who told the agent he didn't do historical novels? To which the agent replied, "It wasn't one when I sent it in."

—Michael Larsen, literary agent and author of *How to Write a Book Proposal*

Most editors generally can't recognize bad writing when they read it. Nor do they try very hard to learn to recognize it.

—Alfred Knopf, cofounder of the Alfred A. Knopf publishing house, now an imprint of Random House

Your agent must absolutely **love your work** to represent it effectively.

➤ No agent can sell your manuscript. An agent can only represent your manuscript. The manuscript must sell itself.

➤ No agent, no matter how skilled or experienced or well connected, can sell a lousy manuscript (unless, of course, the writer is already famous).

➤ Much of the editing and hand-holding once done by editors at large publishing houses is now done by agents and book doctors.

**Don't begrudge an agent her fee.** Really, would you want to do what an agent does for a living?

**An effective editor** reads on behalf of all her readers—and is equally hard to please.

➤ Well-seasoned editors represent their readers effectively. That's how they get to be well-seasoned.

➤ Editors are not the enemy. They want the same thing you want—a good book.

➤ In most publishing houses, an editor's job is to acquire publishable work, not to create it.

Having an agent does not relieve the writer of the responsibilities of marketing.

# GETTING OVER THE TRANSOM

Denise and I have never met. Never networked at a writers conference. Never chatted on the telephone or the Internet. Yet she assigned me to write a monthly how-to column for a newsletter she edited.

Our relationship began when I noticed an item about her newsletter in a writer's magazine. I requested guidelines and a sample issue. I submitted my work over the transom*.

Denise declined the first two articles I sent her but responded with handwritten notes. On my third try, acceptance!

---

\* Many offices used to have a window above the door called a transom, and it was often tilted open at night for ventilation. Legend has it that developing writers, without an agent or industry contacts, would submit their work by throwing it through the open transom after hours.

After that, she continued to turn down some queries and accept others. We kept in touch.

Two years after our initial contact, Denise invited me to create a how-to column for the newsletter. I stumbled a bit at first, but she kept me on track. One by one, for eighteen months, the columns were written and published until Denise shut down the newsletter.

As important as personal relationships are in the writing business, publication is not merely a matter of who you know. The door to publishing can be opened with persistence, professionalism, and good writing. Denise and I still haven't met.

Far more often than not, **editors are right** when they spot a problem. But it remains the writer's job to figure out how to fix it.

➤ Never take your professional relationships for granted—not with editors, not with agents, not with publishers. Freshen those relationships with every new moon.

# STRATEGY:
# FINDING AN AGENT

The best time to identify a prospective agent is before you need one.

I met my agent, Rita Rosenkranz, at the 2000 Columbus Writer's Conference. Though I was not seeking representation at the time, I was screening prospective agents. I attended Rita's sessions and was impressed with her no-nonsense approach. Three years later when I needed an agent, I called Rita.

Well before you've finished writing your book, attend conferences, publishing luncheons—anywhere an agent will be speaking. After a couple of sessions, you'll get an idea of what you want in an agent, and you can gauge a prospective agent's passion for your type of writing—and the agent's receptivity to developing writers—by hearing the agent respond to questions.

The time to start the process is now.

➤ Do not worry that an editor might steal your work. Why would an editor risk it when he or she can buy it on the cheap?

➤ When submitting nonfiction, always give your editor more than is expected by providing sidebars, charts, ideas for graphics, photographs, etc.

You may have to kiss a lot of editorial frogs before you find your publishing prince.

What the writer sees as a final draft, **the editor sees as a working draft.**

➤ Editors read all day and half the night: Neatness counts. Format counts. Spelling counts. Grammar counts. Punctuation counts. Diction counts. Syntax counts. Everything counts.

- Never argue with an editor over a rejection or a killed assignment. Save your ammo for arguing about the writing on the next assignment.

- Never presume to tell an editor how your work should be presented in print. If an editor invites your suggestions, feign ignorance.

Your writing may have been graded on a scale when you were in school, but with editors it's strictly pass/fail.

An editor should tell the author his writing is better than it is. Not a lot better, a little better.

—T. S. Eliot, Nobel Prize-winning poet

It's the old catch-22; you can never get an agent unless you're published, and when you most need one, you can't have one.

—C. J. Cherryh, author of *Explorer* and *Chanur's Legacy*

Editors are extremely fallible people, all of them. Don't put too much trust in them.

—Maxwell Perkins, noted editor

My role, as I see it, is to be the writer's best reader.

—Faith Sale, noted fiction editor

An editor's love for the writing is always seven font sizes greater than his or her **love for the writer.**

> E-mail, the Internet, and fax machines have made it possible for writers and editors to do at the last minute what they used to do in a timely manner.

➤ If one editor calls you a donkey, forget it. If every editor calls you a donkey, learn to pull a cart.

➤ Never mention a book idea to a publisher or an agent unless you're prepared to give the full pitch. Otherwise, you've squandered an opportunity.

Every editor you work with will be
**overworked and underpaid—**
just like you.

Editors and agents troll for new talent at writers conferences. Attend at least one a year, **and swim toward the bait.**

# SELLING YOUR BOOK:

## The Private Joy of Being Published

# By the time I sold my first novel I had learned it was impossible to do so.

—Sarah Willis, award-winning novelist and workshop instructor

What's the secret to getting an agent or publisher? Write a good book.

—Steven Taylor Goldsberry, author of *The Writer's Book of Wisdom*

Don't be thin-skinned or easily discouraged, because it's an odds-long proposition; all of the arts are. Many are called, few are chosen, but it might be you.

—John Updike, Pulitzer Prize-winning author of *Rabbit Is Rich* and *Rabbit at Rest*

> Writers focus on style. Readers focus on content. Publishers focus on readers.

A book written for everyone is a book **written for no one.**

➤ Every book category exists because somebody wrote a book that didn't fit into any of the existing categories.

➤ Small publishing houses are likely to edit your book more carefully, produce it more artfully, and keep it in print longer.

Devote less energy **to finding your niche** and more energy **to creating it.**

Let **emotion** drive your creative endeavors and **intellect** drive your business endeavors.

➤ Take every opportunity to network with editors, publishers, fellow writers, and agents. But you don't need to know someone to get published. The front door is unlocked. You only need open it.

# STRATEGY:
## IDENTIFYING PROSPECTIVE PUBLISHERS

If you do not yet have a literary agent, or if you choose not to use one, you can submit your manuscript to most publishing houses other than the huge conglomerates.

When your manuscript is ready to go to market, or even somewhat earlier, browse bookstores or surf the Internet to identify publishers who release similar kinds of books. Write for each publisher's submission guidelines and current catalog, or study the publishers' listings in the annual directories like *Writer's Market* to determine if your work fits a specific house.

> Even when you're well on the road to having your book published, there will still be days when you are ready to bag the whole project.

At some point, you have to let your book go to market. Then begin anew to write the book you really **meant to write**.

Readers, editors, and publishers always **want more of the same ...** only different.

➤ Publishers are less willing to take a chance on a second book, even if it is better than your first, if the first sold poorly. So promote the heck out of that first book.

However much a publisher does on behalf of your book, it will **never seem like enough.**

# STRATEGY:
## POLISH YOUR PLATFORM

In your book proposal, be sure to include a statement about how you will help market your book. Yep, that's right. Not only do you have to write the darn thing, you have to help sell it, too.

Every publishing house wants to publish books likely to recoup the publisher's investment and then some. Quite simply, a proposal that spells out the author's role in helping to promote a book is more likely to be supported than one that does not.

Your book proposal should present a platform, e.g., a set of venues from which you will launch your book. Your platform may include mailing lists (surface and e-mail), professional associations, your Web site and referrals, club memberships, speaking engagements, media contacts, travel schedule, and anything else that might provide an opportunity to promote your book.

# All good writing is swimming under water and holding your breath.

—F. Scott Fitzgerald, author of *This Side of Paradise*

If only there were a perfect word I could give you—a word like some artichoke that could sit on the table, dry, and become itself.

—Sandra Hochman, author, poet, and documentary filmmaker

It is what is left over when everything explainable has been explained that makes a story worth writing and reading.

—Flannery O'Connor, author of *A Good Man Is Hard to Find*

# Your reputation as a writer is redefined with every piece you publish.

➤ Publishers rarely buy a manuscript for what it is, but rather for what it might become. That's why, when you finally sell a manuscript, the work begins all over again.

➤ If you want to be a commercial success, you must be willing to make changes in your writing solely to enhance its salability.

# The private joy of being published

seeps into one's being over time and colors all subsequent events.

# REJECTION:

## You Become a Writer When You Write

# Rejected pieces aren't failures; unwritten pieces are.

—Greg Daugherty, author and magazine editor

There are two wrong reactions to a rejection slip: deciding it's a final judgment on your story and/or talent, and deciding it's no judgment on your story and/or talent.

—Nancy Kress, author of *Characters, Emotion & Viewpoint*

Never buy an editor or publisher a lunch or a drink until he has bought an article, story, or book from you. This rule is absolute and may be broken only at your peril.

—John Creasey, author of *The Touch of Death* and *Prophet of Fire*

# A letter of rejection is an opinion, not a judgment.

Each time you receive a rejection slip, you are one step closer to finding **the right market** for your work.

➤ When you get a rejection slip, congratulate yourself. You can't get rejected unless you're writing and submitting your work.

➤ Your work may be rejected for reasons having nothing to do with you, your writing, or the worth of the project. And usually there's no way of knowing.

➤ Ultimately, you must trust your own judgment—not that of the marketplace—when determining the worth of your writing.

➤ Temper your enthusiasm over an acceptance and your disappointment over a rejection—it usually represents the opinion of only one or two people.

If you've been buried in rejections and rained on with criticism, **it's time to bloom!**

> For well-written work, each rejection slip represents an error in submission, nothing more.

Every rejection slip adds to your knowledge about the right **market for your work.**

# MISTAKES, MISTAKES

Over a period of months, I had been touched by my widowed mother's efforts to "get rid of the clutter" around her house. If one of her children or grandchildren commented on a book or wall hanging, Mom would immediately offer it as a gift. Moved by her efforts, I dashed off a personal essay. I wrote with emotion and integrity. I wrote from the heart.

I sent the piece off to an editor who had previously published my work. In declining the piece, he noted it was well written but didn't go anywhere. I missed the point and submitted the essay to two

other editors. Both declined, but commented favorably on the writing. All three editors noted the essay lacked a point for the
reader. Finally, I woke up and rewrote it.

There is not one writing lesson here,
but three. First, why did I submit the
piece without letting it breathe? I know
better than that.

Second, why did I submit a personal
essay without making a point for the
reader? I know better than that.

Third, why did I have to hear from
three experienced editors that the essay
needed direction? I know better than that.

Don't you make the same mistakes.
*You* know better than that.

# STRATEGY:
## TARGET YOUR SUBMISSIONS

One of the most common errors in seeking publication is to submit a manuscript or article to a publisher or publication that simply doesn't publish that type of work. Rejection is inevitable.

Don't submit your work to every publication that might use it or, worse yet, to every publication where you'd like your work to appear. Instead, target your submissions. Study a publication's guidelines, which are usually available upon request (and for a self-addressed stamped envelop), posted on a publication's Web site, or listed in an annual directory like *Writer's Market*.

If you're submitting to magazines or journals, study the publications themselves. In your cover letter or query, tell the editor why your piece is right for his or her publication.

A targeted submission is far more likely to hit home.

# A first-rate piece of writing
may not be right for the markets, but
## just right for a contest.

➤ When you receive a rejection slip, reread your work
with a fresh eye. If it still pleases you, send it out
again—the same day.

➤ If your work is rejected nine times out of ten and
you have material out to twenty markets, you have
two acceptances on the way.

An author who claims to write for posterity must be a bad one. **We should never know** for whom we write.

—E. M. Cioran, author of *The Trouble With Being Born*

The problem is not whether the song will continue, but whether a dark space can be found where the notes can resonate.

—Rainer Maria Rilke, author of *Duino Elegies*

Now I live only in the company of a few disobedient words.

—Karl Krolow, German poet

If you are in difficulties with a book, try the element of surprise; attack it at an hour when it isn't expecting it.

—H. G. Wells, author of *The War of the Worlds*

➤ If your goal is to create publishable writing, it doesn't matter whether you generate three rejections for every acceptance, or thirty.

➤ When an editor declines your submission, don't take it personally. Reread, rewrite, reslant, and take it somewhere else.

A well-written book may be rejected simply because an agent or publisher cannot project a sufficient market for it.

# STRATEGY:
# SEND THANK-YOU NOTES

If a publisher declines your book proposal, consider sending a thank-you note (handwritten if your penmanship is legible) or e-mail. In it, ask if the publisher might refer you to another prospective publisher. (This works best if the publisher sends you a personalized rejection letter. If you receive a form reject letter, it's best just to move on.) This is how I was directed to Writer's World Press, who published the 1998 edition of *The Writer's Little Instruction Book*.

By the way, sending handwritten thank-you notes to editors, publishers, and agents who decline your work is an excellent way to build a network of friends in the business. These folks hardly ever get thank-you notes of any kind, let alone from writers whose work they have declined.

**You become a writer when you write**—not when someone decides your writing will be published.

# PROMOTION &
# BOOK TOURS:

## Relish in the Process

> I believe what makes books sell, more than anything else, is word of mouth.
>
> —Nora Ephron, screenwriter

> The profession of book-writing makes horse racing seem like a solid, stable business.
>
> —John Steinbeck, Nobel Prize-winning novelist

> Someday I hope to write a book where the royalties will pay for the copies I give away.
>
> —Clarence Darrow, trial lawyer and writer

> A person who publishes a book appears willfully in public with his pants down.
>
> —Edna St. Vincent Millay, Pulitzer Prize-winning poet

## Whatever you think is over the top in book promotion ... isn't.

➤ Writing a book is thin-lipped determination.
Getting a book published is vocal persistence.
Promoting a book is screaming madness.

➤ In promoting your book, think orchestra,
not shotgun.

> In publishing, the key question is, "Who is going to buy this?"

Your book must be strong enough **to sell to strangers.** Not friends. Not relatives. Not colleagues.

Everything you do to gain favorable notice for your book **is part of marketing.**

> For every ten promotional efforts you make on behalf of your book, perhaps one will pay off. But you never know which one.

Never give away a copy of your book to anyone who might buy it— **except maybe your mother.**

➤ A national book tour, arranged and paid for by the publisher, is as unlikely as a polished first draft. More likely, the publisher will ask you to share travel costs or piggyback signings onto your personal travel.

➤ The best way to keep your sanity while trying to sell a book is to start writing the next one.

➤ Most developing writers do not know the hard truths about marketing books. It's just as well.

Congratulations! Your book is about to be published. Now you have to **sell the darn thing.**

> Writing is a quiet business. Book promotion is a loud business.

If your novel has **a really satisfying ending,** chances are the reader will scurry out to buy another of your books.

# WHAT, NO WINE
AND CHEESE?

One spring day in Memphis, I arrived at the mall just a few minutes before my afternoon signing was scheduled to begin. I spotted the bookstore right away and counted myself lucky for choosing that entrance to the mall.

I was disappointed, but not particularly surprised, to see no indication they expected me. No table set up, no posters announcing my signing, no copies of my book in sight. *Ah, well.*

I introduced myself to a sales clerk, who turned me over to the assistant manager, who scrambled into the back room to locate my books. Ten minutes later, the assistant manager emerged empty-handed. He asked, "Are you sure you're in the right bookstore?"

It hit me like a ton of books. I was supposed to be at a competing bookstore in the same mall.

No matter how well-prepared you are, no matter how well-rested, somewhere along the line you will screw it up. Make amends, forgive yourself, and move on.

➤ You will have to give up something in order to make time to promote your book.

➤ Promotion is an insatiable beast. You will never be able to do all that is possible to promote your book.

**The best salesperson** for your book is you. Not your agent, not the publisher, not the publisher's rep. **You.**

# The smaller the publisher, the more of the promotional load **you'll have to shoulder.**

—Blythe Camenson and Marshall J. Cook, coauthors of *Give 'Em What They Want*

The only time you can safely stop promoting your books is when you're ready to stop writing them.
—Jay Conrad Levinson, Rick Frishman, and Michael Larsen, coauthors of *Guerrilla Marketing for Writers*

An audience is never wrong. An individual member of it may be an imbecile, but a thousand imbeciles together in the dark—that is central genius.
—Billy Wilder, Academy Award-winning director and screenwriter

When a bookseller recommends a book, it's called handselling. Your book tour will build the relationships that generate handselling—**and restocking.**

➤ Never schedule a book signing to conflict with a local football game or a crafts show.

➤ Before your first book signing, draft at least three sample inscriptions (a personal message you write to accompany your autograph). Perhaps you'll want to use a key phrase from your book.

The idea of a **book tour** is not to meet your audience, but to **create it.**

Do give a free copy to anyone willing to promote your book. Everyone else **should buy it.**

➤ When you're doing a signing, don't expect someone to be there to hold your hand and faun over you, unless you bring along your own personal hand-holder (which may not a bad idea).

> Your reception at the bookstore will vary from wine and cheese, balloons, fresh flowers, linen tablecloths, and scented candles to "What's your book again?"

Be prepared for a wide **variety of responses** to you and your book. Ignore the negative ones, they likely have nothing to do with you.

## SIGN HERE PLEASE

While I was on a book tour, the owner of a bookstore in Blytheville, Arkansas, asked me to sign one of her folding wooden chairs. I had been told that this was John Grisham's favorite bookstore. Sure enough, there among the dozen or so signed chairs was one signed by John Grisham. Alas, all the slats on that chair were already spoken for. I signed my name on one of the other chairs.

Great fun, this writing biz. Quirky things will happen. Marvelous things will happen. Relish these moments.

You earned them.

- Be prepared for light traffic at book signings. There is no way of predicting success, but weekends are better than weekdays.

- There is no optimal time for a book signing, other than not at the dinner hour.

**Rainy days** draw more customers to book signings than **sunny days**.

It's easier to write about those you hate—just as it's **easier to criticize** a bad play or **a bad book**.

—Dorothy Parker, short-story writer and poet

Most writers worry about getting an editor to like their work. They forget that the book actually needs to sell off the bookstore shelves.

—Anne Kinsman Fisher, author of *The Legend of Tommy Morris*

Anyone can sell. The secret is to have 50,000 books in your basement.

—Mary Ellen Pinkham, author of *Mary Ellen's Complete Home Reference Book*

> The more useful or **intriguing a presentation** you can offer at a signing, the better the draw.

➤ Sit, don't stand. Make eye contact and greet passersby with, "Hi, I'm signing my book today!"

➤ Make no assumptions about who will buy your book. Make yourself approachable to everyone.

Wear a "Visiting Author" **name tag** as you walk through the mall en route to your book signing and whenever you take a break.

➤ During your signing, loan the bookstore one or two counter displays with a photo of you and/or your book cover and the caption, "Have you met our visiting author?"

# STRATEGY:
# THIS LITTLE WRITER WENT TO MARKET

For every two hours of writing, spend an hour marketing and promoting yourself and your work. If that seems like a lot of work, it is. As part of your marketing efforts, you should:

➤ Stay current with the industry by reading print and online journals like Publishers Weekly.
➤ Identify and research prospective publishers by browsing bookstores and the Internet.
➤ Submit your finished work to the prospective publishers you researched.
➤ Sell your published work to readers (in-person selling is still the best).
➤ Raise your profile by participating in regional events.
➤ Sniff out assignments and new projects.

## Mail a handwritten thank-you note to your contact in the bookstore after each signing.

➤ Casinos sometimes use shills to attract players to empty gaming tables. One or two friends examining your book and talking about it will help draw passersby to your table at a book signing.

➤ Think not about how much more grand it might have been. Be grateful for your readers and for bookstores.

**Relish in the process.** You are doing what you dreamed of doing as you wrote the book.

# READERS & WRITERS:

## Listen Like a Sponge; Read Like a Predator

There are worse crimes than burning books. One of them is **not reading them.**

—Joseph Brodsky, Nobel Prize-winning poet

If you don't read for pleasure, you'll lose your edge as a writer.

—Nora Roberts, author of *Winner Takes All*

Most writers, you know, are awful sticks to talk with.

—Sherwood Anderson, author of *Winesburg, Ohio*

Anything that is written to please the author is worthless.

—Blaise Pascal, French mathematician, philosopher, and writer

# Stories are windows through which we look at the world.

➤ The reality created by the human mind while reading is unmatched by any technology.

➤ The writer must keep every promise to the reader, though perhaps not in the way the reader expected.

Viewers invite television into their homes. Readers invite writers into their minds.

# Trust the reader to get it.

➤ Only one person at a time will read your work. Write for one reader, not an audience.

➤ Writing is a partnership: Hold hands with your reader's imagination.

➤ Write not to lead your reader to answers, but to questions.

> Seduced,
the reader
continues,
into the
night.

A writer's words
may offer pearls of
wisdom, but 'tis
**the reader**
who threads them
into a necklace.

## BROWSERS ASK THE DARNDEST QUESTIONS

Browsers at book signings often ask, "Have you written anything else?" Or, "How much is your book?" Some will mistake you for a store employee and ask if you have a certain book in stock. They will also ask, "Are these free?" and "Where are the restrooms?" One prospective customer looked over multiple copies of my book and asked, "Did you write all these books?" Honest. But my favorite customer question at signings, asked more often than you would suppose, is, "Did you write this book?"

> Revere the reader, for the reader allows the writer access to his or her most private sanctuaries: the mind and the heart.

Better to assume the **reader is smarter** than you are than the other way around.

# Good fiction insists on being continued after the last paragraph.

➤ People love to read about themselves. The writer's job is to convince them that's what they're doing.

➤ People love to look into others' lives—especially if the others aren't aware of it.

➤ Readers don't want to hear about your life. They want to hear about their life, as it might be.

➤ Readers love to see someone struggle against all odds, succeed, and grow in the process. It gives them hope for real life.

➤ In a good novel, the book changes the protagonist. In an exceptional novel, the book changes the reader.

Readers love bad news—as long as it's about someone else.

Readers don't want merely to read your story; they want to **experience it.**

> **Readers love a good series—familiarity breeds contentment.**

**Shared experience** is the basis for every writer-reader relationship.

## FOR HER COLLECTION

About 10 percent of the customers at a book signing buy a book on title alone. They say "Oh" as soon as they see it, flip through the pages without reading, and ask the writer to sign it. Not 10 percent of the browsers, mind you, but 10 percent of the customers.

Attempting to engage one such customer in conversation, I asked if she was a writer. "No," she responded. I asked if she was buying the book as a gift. Again, "No." After a pause she added, "I collect signed books."

## The reality created by the writer is defined by the reader.

➤ A book lives its truest life not in the writer's mind, but in the reader's.

➤ Stories reflect a writer's limits. Readers explode those limits.

➤ Readers bring to a story a willingness to suspend disbelief—but not a willingness to abandon credibility.

# The first draft
is for the writer.
Every draft thereafter
is for the reader.

➤ The writer's gift is the exercise of other people's imagination.

➤ When you, as the writer, reveal a bit of yourself to the reader, a bit of the reader is revealed, as well.

The reader (and the critics) will always see **more than you wrote**.

**A good story is never finished.**
**Each time it's read, it's created anew.**

➤ **Readers asks three questions:**

  ➤ Who are these people?
  ➤ Could this happen?
  ➤ Why should I care?

**The writer's trick is to answer these questions**
**before the reader asks them.**

> Your work, for better or for worse, will never speak to all readers in quite the same way.

Even a first-rate piece of writing **will not speak to all readers.**

➤ Write every story as if it were the only story of yours the reader will ever experience. Write every sentence as if it were the only sentence of yours the reader will ever read.

➤ Readers, bless them, will worry about almost anything. Be sure to give them something to worry about.

Readers of fiction want you to **deceive them**. All they ask is that you be good at it.

Writers aspire to create an empathetic audience, but **any audience** will do.

# A writer's worst sin is **to bore the reader.**

➤ Read every day, without apology.

➤ To write well, read well.

➤ Read like an editor. If you don't know how to read like an editor, pretend you are a shopkeeper examining a bill of sale.

A book is a version of the world. If you do not like it, ignore it; or offer **your own version in return.**

—Salman Rushdie, author of *Midnight's Children*

A good book is the precious lifeblood of a master spirit, embalmed and treasured up on a purpose to a life beyond a life.

—John Milton, author of *Paradise Lost*

The good of a book lies in its being read. A book is made up of signs that speak of other signs, which in their turn speak of things.

—Umberto Eco, Italian critic and novelist

To understand why **we write,** we must first understand why **we read.**

> ➤ The writer who reads the masters is more likely to become one.

The writer who understands **why people read** will understand how to write.

➤ To grow as a writer, you must grow as a reader.

➤ There is good and bad in every piece of writing, though sometimes you have to look a might hard.

➤ One of the graces of reading a writer for the first time is to be unaware of the writer's potential.

➤ The only way to develop an eye for written language is to read voraciously.

➤ Reading is a writer's on-the-job training.

➤ Read the kind of writing you like to write. And read stuff that is wildly different from your usual interests.

Write the book you would love to read—and would be willing to **pay good money for**.

Read as a writer, and write as a reader.

As you read, consider how the writer **evoked a response** in you, how he or she motivated you to take action.

➤ As you develop as a writer, continue to read about writing. You will remind yourself of basic tenets and discover new meaning in familiar advice.

# Reading shapes who we are; writing shapes who we become.

➤ Your body says, "You are what you eat."
Your mind says, "You are what you read."
Your soul says, "You are what you write."

➤ Let your passion for reading inform your passion for writing.

# STRATEGY:
## GETTING TO KNOW YOUR AUDIENCE

At every public appearance, pass around a sign-up sheet inviting participants to join your mailing list. Ask for both e-mail and surface mail addresses, but be happy with whatever you get. (Note the date and location of the event on each set of addresses.)

Over time, you'll create a mailing list for e-mail or surface mail notifications, or perhaps you'll produce a newsletter. This will give you another plank in your marketing platform for all future writing, and you'll have a better feel for who your audience is and what they want.

> Whether you're reading or writing, a good book has a life that won't let you live your own.

# Reading is never a waste of time, especially for a writer.

You must write about people who touch the reader; you must **make the reader care.**

—John Irving, author of *The Cider House Rules*

If your reader doesn't understand what you're saying, you're talking to yourself.

—Nigel Hamilton, British historian and biographer

A few times in every story I simply can't resist the urge to peek around the corner and wiggle my ears at the reader.

—Lee K. Abbott, author of *Dreams of Distant Lives*

➤ Being a writer robs you of the joy of reading solely for pleasure. Every book you read becomes an object lesson.

➤ Reading is more likely to influence your work through osmosis than epiphany.

Read in order to live. Write in order to live fully.

We first **learn to write by reading**. It pretty much stays that way all through a career.

➤ For a child, reading is the ultimate escape. For an adult, writing is the ultimate escape.

➤ A lifetime of reading is a necessary-but-not-sufficient condition for writing.

Listen like a sponge.
Read like a predator.

# ABOUT THE AUTHOR

Paul Raymond Martin has published more than three hundred stories, poems, and articles. He is the author of *Writer's Little Instruction Book: Inspiration & Motivation*, *Writer's Little Instruction Book: Craft & Technique*, and *Writer's Little Instruction Book: Getting Published*, all from Writer's Digest Books.

Paul lives on a seventy-acre farm in northwestern Pennsylvania, where he leases the fields to a neighboring farmer. When he's not writing, Paul likes to play in the dirt and raise wormy apples.